Where Is Dad's Phone?

By Cameron Macintosh

"Where is my phone?"
said Dad.

"I can not see it."

"We do not have the phone,"
said Phil and Quin.

"Let's hunt for Dad's phone, Quin," said Phil.

Quin and Phil hunted.

Dad's phone was not
in Mum's big bag.

It was not in Dad's mug
of pens.

Phil hunted in Mum's shed.

Quin looked in Dad's
red box.

"Let's look in Ned's cat bed," said Phil.

Quin looked in Ned's bed.

"Here is the phone!" Quin yelled.

"What was it in Ned's bed for?" said Dad.

Ned hid in his bed.

Dad looked at his phone.

"I can see some photos
on it!" Dad said.
"Look at Ned!"

"Ned is in **all** the photos!"
said Phil.
"What a fun cat!"

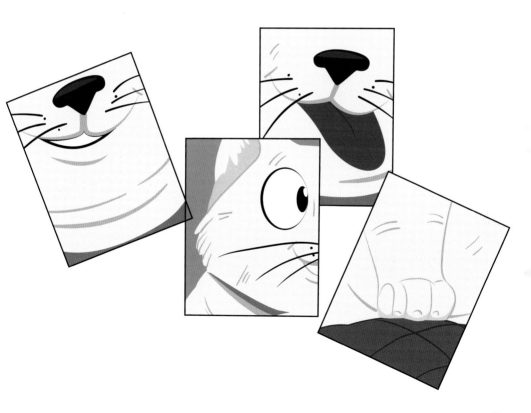

CHECKING FOR MEANING

1. Where did Phil and Quin look for Dad's phone in the house? *(Literal)*

2. Where did they look in Mum's shed? *(Literal)*

3. Why do you think Ned is in all the photos? *(Inferential)*

EXTENDING VOCABULARY

phone	Look at the word *phone*. What sound does it start with? Can you find another word in the book that starts with the same sound?
hunt	What do you do if you *hunt* for something? What is another word you could use that has the same meaning? E.g. search, seek.
photos	What is a *photo*? How can we take a photo? What can we do with a photo that we have taken?

MOVING BEYOND THE TEXT

1. How have phones changed over the years?

2. Who do you talk to on the phone? What do you talk about?

3. Discuss how the phone got to be in Ned's bed.

4. Why do people like taking and keeping photos?

SPEED SOUNDS

sh	ch	th	th	wh	qu	ph
		voiced	unvoiced			

PRACTICE WORDS

Quin

Phil

shed